AN ATLAS OF AFRICA

AN ATLAS OF AFRICA

by

J. F. HORRABIN

LONDON
VICTOR GOLLANCZ LTD
1960

Printed in Great Britain by
The Camelot Press Ltd., London and Southampton

PREFACE

THIS BOOK IS NOT intended for the specialist. My aim has been to provide for the intelligent newspaper-reader a summary of some of the key facts about one of the great "burning problems" of today. Nor does it pretend to be objective. It has been drawn and written in the fixed conviction that Europeans owe Africans a big debt; and that the doctrine of *apartheid* and the "settler mentality" are uncivilised, un-Christian and altogether damnable.

I want to express my thanks for generous help received from Basil Davidson (who will probably groan with pain at the inadequacy of my prehistory), M. Akram Bayatti, Austen Albu, M.P., Sir Leslie Plummer, M.P., and Dr. Anthony Michaelis (for stimulating suggestions). Also to my wife and to Dorothy Davies for their invaluable help in preparing the text.

J. F. H.

Hendon,
    July, 1959

CONTENTS

CONTENTS

CONTENTS

PART I

BACKGROUND

MAP 1

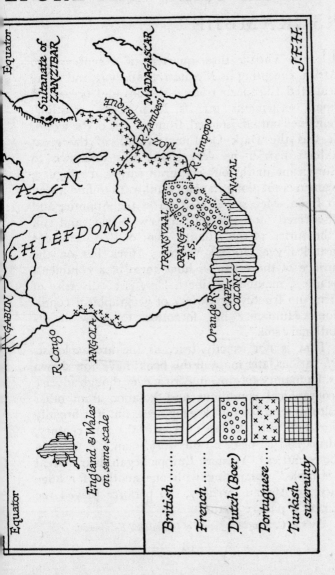

J.F.H.

Equator

Sultanate of ZANZIBAR

MADAGASCAR

R. Zambesi

A   N

CHIEFDOMS

GABUN

R. Congo

ANGOLA

MOÇAMBIQUE

R. Limpopo

TRANSVAAL

ORANGE F.S.

NATAL

Orange R.

CAPE COLONY

Equator

England & Wales on same scale

British ....

French ....

Dutch (Boer) ....

Portuguese .....

Turkish suzerainty

BEFORE THE "SCRAMBLE"

UNTIL ABOUT three-quarters of a century ago
Africa, excepting its Mediterranean shore and many
scattered European trading-stations and occasional
small settlements on its long ocean coastline,
remained cut off, isolated, from the rest of the world.
It was the Dark Continent. South of the great
Sahara barrier its very shape was unknown to
Europeans until, four centuries earlier, Portuguese
seamen crept along its coast southward to find a way
to India. Men sailed west across the Atlantic, and
discovered (and peopled) a New World; and still
"the Africa of the Atlantic slept on." An eminent
historical-geographer[1] wrote—"Africa lies on the
surface of the ocean, a huge torso of a continent,
headless, memberless, inert. Here is no diversity of
form, no fructifying variety of geographical conditions. Humanity has forgotten to grow in its
stationary soil."

That is not exactly true, as the archaeologists
(*cf.* various later maps in this book) have now shown
us. Humanity *did* grow in Africa, even though adverse
geographical conditions and isolation from other
cultures retarded full development. But it is broadly
true that, until the last quarter of the 19th century,
Africa had no place on the world-map. Then, when
the countries of Western Europe began their "Great
Scramble," competing with one another for huge
slices of African territory, she perforce played the
part of a passive victim.

[1] E. C. Semple, *Influences of Geographical Environment.*

Let us begin our story with two maps illustrating this opening of the modern chapter of African history, going back afterwards to the preceding chapters.

Map No. 1 shows Africa—as known to, and in contact with, Europeans—in 1870. The north-eastern corner of the continent—Egypt, Tripoli, and the Red Sea coast—was part of the Turkish Empire. French, Portuguese, and British had established themselves at various points on the coast, west, east and south; their "influence" extending but a few miles into the hinterland. The French had already begun to colonise Algeria, and the Dutch had pushed north from the Cape, away from British rule, and established the two Boer republics. American philanthropists had purchased a piece of territory (Liberia) on the west coast and peopled it with freed slaves. Abyssinia (Ethiopia) and Morocco had kept a precarious independence. The vast interior of the continent was "empty."

That is, it contained only Africans.

MAP 2

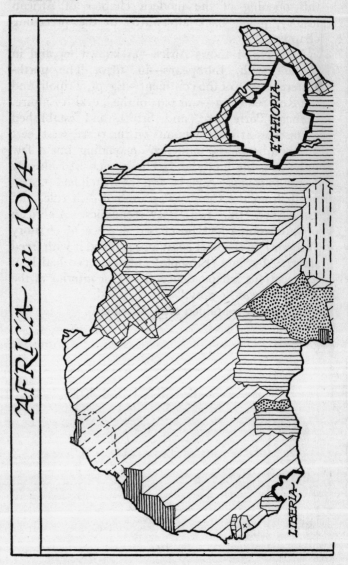

AFRICA in 1914

THE GREAT SCRAMBLE

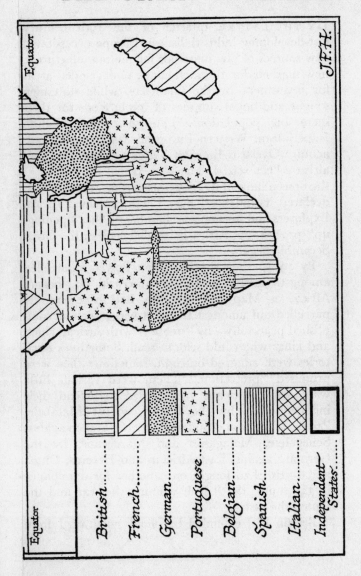

Equator

Equator

J.F.H.

British..........
French..........
German..........
Portuguese..........
Belgian..........
Spanish..........
Italian..........
Independent
States..........

THE GREAT SCRAMBLE

BY THE LATTER quarter of the 19th century fast-developing industrialism in Europe necessitated new sources of raw materials for the manufacturers, new markets for the merchants, undeveloped areas for investment by the financiers, while statesmen sought additional supplies of staple foods for their increasing populations. Thus was born Modern Imperialism. Western European States must needs acquire Overseas Empires. Large parts of Asia had already been seized. The New World of America— the descendants of its European settlers, that is—had declared its independence. There remained Africa. Explorers and missionaries had begun the "opening-up" process. So, Africa being defenceless, the Great Scramble began.

By 1914, when the European Powers quarrelled among themselves and the First World War began, Africa, as Map No. 2 shows, had been entirely parcelled out amongst them. It was largely accomplished peacefully—by "treaties" with African chiefs and kings who could seldom read. Sometimes territories were annexed outright, sometimes they were promised "protection." There were various little wars, when Africans vainly tried to defend their independence; by the British against Matabele, Zulus, Ashantis and Sudanese, by the French against Senegalese, Malagasies and Moroccans, by the Germans against East Africans and Hereros. Dutch and British had fought one another for dominance in the south, the British winning the war and the Dutch the peace.

Britain had extended her hold northward from

the Cape to beyond the Zambesi and southward from Egypt (taken over from the Turks). There were visions of an all-British Cape to Cairo railway. France had pressed eastward from Senegal and Guinea across the whole breadth of Sahara and Sudan. The two "new" European Powers, Italy and Germany, had joined in the Scramble. Italy had ousted Turkey from Tripoli (Libya) and secured two areas on the borders of Ethiopia, having failed in an attempt to conquer that country. Germany held four areas, west and east. Little Belgium, whose King Leopold had backed Stanley's exploration of the Congo basin, ruled a vast area in the middle of the continent.

Now, indeed, Africa figured on the modern map.

MAP 3

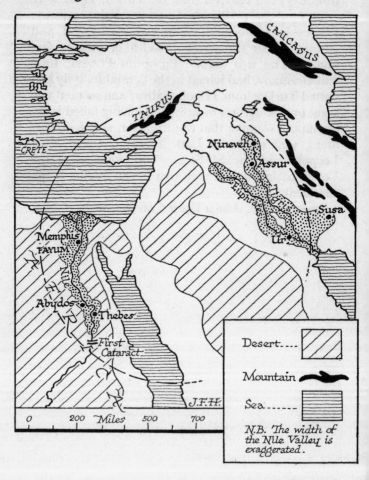

CAUCASUS

TAURUS

CRETE

Nineveh
Assur
Euphrates
Tigris
Susa
Ur

Memphis
FAYUM
Nile
Abydos
Thebes
First Cataract

J.F.H.

0   200   Miles   500   700

Desert.....

Mountain

Sea......

N.B. The width of
the Nile Valley is
exaggerated.

24

CRADLES OF
CIVILISATION

WE GO BACK 6000 years, to the first beginnings
of any recorded African history. Western civilisation
began in the fertile valleys of the Nile, in north-east
Africa, and of the Tigris and Euphrates, in western
Asia—two areas not far distant from one another;
in a single "region," though academically classified
as in different continents. Why were men here able
to make the technological and social advances which
formed the basis of civilised life? Why in Egypt
rather than anywhere else in Africa? Why, having
taken root here, did not civilisation spread over the
rest of Africa—instead of north and west to Europe?

The brief answer is:—favourable geographical
conditions. In the Nile Valley there was exceptionally fertile soil, which the seasonal flooding of
the river not merely kept fertile, but made its
extension possible by man-made irrigation. This
entailed a more and more highly organised society.
"The exploitation of the Nile Valley," says Gordon
Childe, "required exceptionally close social co-
operation." Secondly, natural protection against
marauders and invaders was provided by the
surrounding desert. Egypt, in effect, was a long,
narrow island, cut off by natural barriers from the
rest of the world. It was these barriers which
hindered the spread of Egyptian civilisation to the
great mass of the continent; and it was this isolation
which kept that civilisation relatively static for so
many centuries.

MAP 4

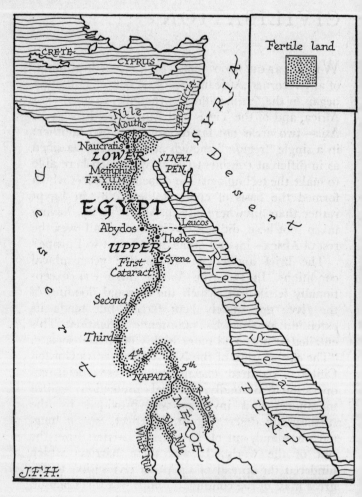

ANCIENT EGYPT

We have no space here for even a brief summary of Egyptian history. The first Pharaoh reigned in the 5th millennium B.C. Since its conquest by Alexander the Great (4th century B.C.) Egypt, until our own day, has never been ruled by Egyptians— Greeks, Romans, Arabs, Turks, French and British have succeeded each other as governments in the Nile Valley.

Egypt's natural isolation, as we have seen, limited the influence of its civilisation on the rest of Africa. When men learned navigation they carried that influence from the Nile mouth across the Mediterranean to the island of Crete. But it spread only slowly and weakly from Upper Egypt up the river to Napata and Meroë, and along the Red Sea coast. And archaeologists are still debating how far (and how much) it was carried westward across the Libyan desert to the (then) fertile areas in the Sahara.

One point, in view of certain current attitudes to Africans, should be emphasised. The ancient Egyptians were not mentally or in any other respect superior to other Africans. They achieved what they did because of exceptionally favourable geographical conditions at a particular stage of social development.

MAP 5

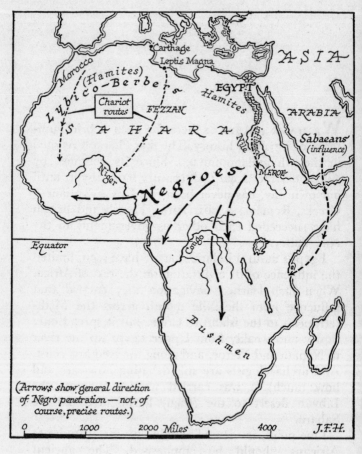

FIRST STEPS FROM
BARBARISM

WHAT OF THE rest of Africa while civilisation
was developing in Egypt? The archaeologists are
only now beginning to trace the social evolution of
the continent—the advance, varying greatly in
different regions, from primitive barbarism to the
Neolithic stage, with agriculture and stone tools, and,
later, the use of iron and the appearance of stone
buildings.

The map attempts to summarise some broad facts
about three or four millennia B.C. Hamitic peoples
occupied the northern part of the continent (parts of
the Sahara were then fertile).

The Negroes had entered Africa from Asia about
6000 or 5000 B.C. and were spreading westward and
southward. Bushmen, probably the continent's
original inhabitants, were being pushed further and
further south. The Phoenicians (see next map)
established their colonies on the Mediterranean in
the 1st millennium B.C. and their influence spread
across the Sahara—stone engravings of this date
showing wheeled chariots have been discovered.

On the eastern side of the continent Sabaean
culture percolated down the coast from southern
Arabia as far as Tanganyika, this also at some time
in the 1st millennium B.C. or early centuries A.D.

MAP 6

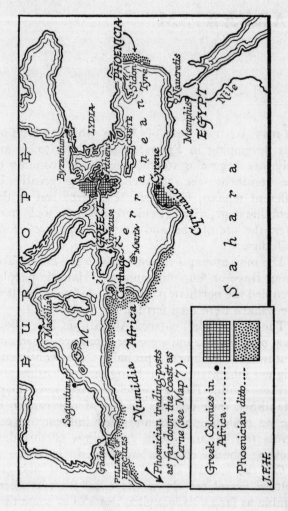

PHOENICIANS AND GREEKS

ONE MIGHT CALL the Phoenicians the first colonialists. After the collapse of Cretan dominance in the eastern Mediterranean (12th century B.C.) they sailed from their home bases of Sidon and Tyre, established themselves in Malta and Sicily, then on the northern coast of Africa, and finally out through the Pillars of Hercules to Gades, in Spain, and Cerne, down the Atlantic coast of Africa. Their main base later was Carthage, in what is now Tunisia, and their settlements extended along almost the whole of the western Mediterranean African coast.

At this time, too, colonies were founded by the Greek city-states in Cyrenaica, opposite the mainland of Greece on the north side of the sea.

Ever since this period Mediterranean Africa has been more closely linked with southern Europe than with Africa south of the Sahara.

MAP 7

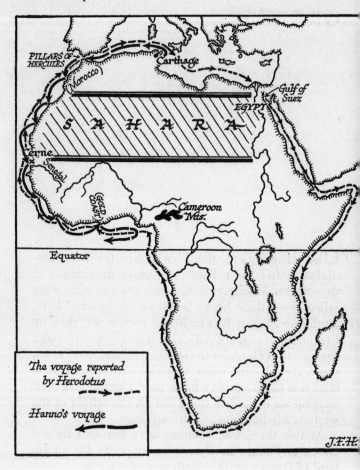

The voyage reported
by Herodotus

Hanno's voyage

THE FIRST
CIRCUMNAVIGATION

About 596 B.C. Phoenician sailors, under orders from Pharaoh Necho of Egypt, set sail from the Gulf of Suez, down the Red Sea, and returned three years later to the Nile mouth through the Pillars of Hercules, having circumnavigated the continent of Africa. Each year, according to Herodotus, they had landed for three months, and grown and harvested a crop. The Cape was not rounded again for 2000 years.

Something under a century later Hanno, a Carthaginian admiral, sailed westward from Carthage with a fleet of 60 ships, carrying 30,000 people, men and women, and established colonies at various points along the African Atlantic coast as far south as Cerne. He took interpreters aboard at each stopping-place, and sailed on until his men were alarmed by the sight of the Cameroon mountain in eruption. Most probably he made one landing on what was later called the Gold Coast (now Ghana).

MAP 8

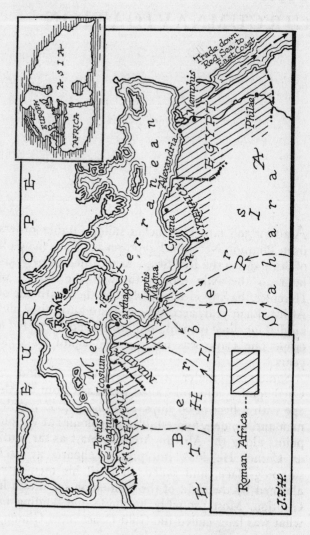

EUROPE

ASIA
EUROPE
AFRICA

Trade down
Red Sea to
East Coast

Memphis
Alexandria
EGYPT
CYRENAICA
Cyrene
Philae

Mediterranean
Leptis Magna
Carthage
ROME
Utica

Sahara

Order

Africa

Numidia
Mediterranea
Portus Magnus
Icosium
MAURETANIA

Berber Hills

BETICA

Roman Africa .....

J.F.H.

34

THE ROMANS IN AFRICA

WHEN THE Romans finally destroyed Carthage in the Third Punic War (146 B.C.) they were on the way to becoming masters of the Mediterranean. They invented a slogan, *"Mare Nostrum,"* which Mussolini revived some 2000 years later. Imperial Rome continued what Republican Rome had begun. Under the Emperor Aurelian (3rd century A.D.) all the African coastlands north of the Sahara, from Mauretania (Morocco) to Egypt, were under Roman rule. "Africa" was the province in the centre (now Tunisia and the western half of Libya). South of the provinces was "Ethiopia." From it, says Sir Mortimer Wheeler,[1] "the cities of the coastal fringe received the products of the interior—ivory, precious stones, gold-dust, ostrich feathers, slaves . . . and above all, animals for the amphitheatres of Rome and elsewhere." This caravan trade made a great step forward when the camel was introduced in the 3rd century A.D.

Sir Mortimer Wheeler also reports evidences of Roman traders down the East Coast (e.g. the finding of Roman coins of different periods in Kenya).

Inset is a map of the world by a Roman geographer showing an Africa much reduced in size, with the southern end of the Red Sea co-terminous with the "furthest south" of the continent.

[1] *Rome Beyond the Imperial Frontiers.*

MAP 9

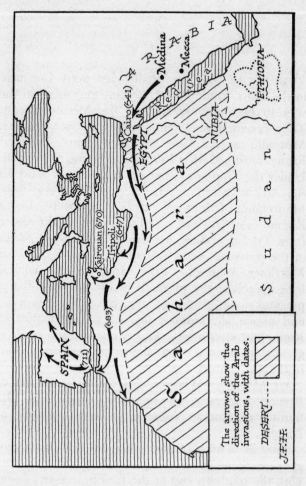

The arrows show the direction of the Arab invasions, with dates.

DESERT----

J.F.H.

36

THE COMING OF ISLAM

Muhammad died in A.D. 632. A century after his death his followers ruled over an empire extending across the whole of North Africa, across the straits and into Spain, as well as all the Middle East, and Asia to the borders of India and China. In all the African lands conquered by the Arabs Arabic to this day remains the dominant language; while the faith of Islam spread south across the desert to areas outside Arab rule. In the coastlands Islam almost completely obliterated all trace of previous religions or cultures. Ever since the conquest, and more than ever today, these have been Arab lands.

Far up the Nile valley, to the south of conquered Egypt, Ethiopia, isolated in her mountains, remained Christian.

MAP 10

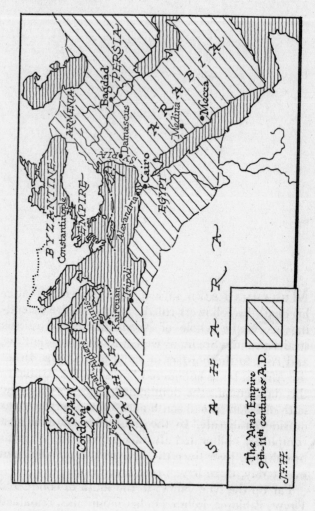

The Arab Empire
9th–11th centuries A.D.

J.F.H.

THE ARAB EMPIRE

"From their peninsula [Arabia]," writes Edward Atiyah,[1] "the Arabs brought two great contributions: Islam and the Arabic language, together with their code of desert chivalry. They also brought the psychological stimulus of their impact, as a vigorous conquering people, on the stagnant, if more civilised inhabitants of the outside world. In this world there was Greek philosophy, Roman ideas of law and government, Byzantine and Persian art, Christian theology and the Judaic tradition. Arab civilisation was a product of all these factors." In its golden age, from the 9th to the 11th century, there were two great centres west and east: Cordova, in Spain, and Bagdad, on the Tigris. During those two hundred years these two cities were perhaps the most important centres of world civilisation. When the Arab empire broke up, Tunis and Cairo were the capitals of kingdoms. Decay set in with the coming of the Ottoman Turks in the 14th-15th centuries. The countries of the Maghreb degenerated into pirate statelets, while Tripoli and Egypt were ruled (or misruled) by Turkish governors.

[1] *The Arabs.*

MAP II

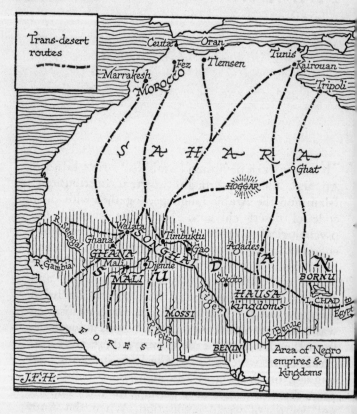

Trans-desert routes

Ceuta · Oran · Tunis · Kairouan
Marrakesh · Fez · Tlemsen · Tripoli
MOROCCO

S A H A R A

HOGGAR · Ghat

R. Senegal · Walata · Timbuktu · Agades
Ghana · Gao · N
GHANA · SONGHAI · BORNU
R. Gambia · Mali · Djenne · Sokoto · L. CHAD · to Egypt
MALI · U · HAUSA kingdoms
MOSSI · Niger
R. Volta · FOREST · BENIN · R. Benue

Area of Negro empires & kingdoms

J.F.H.

KINGDOMS OF THE WESTERN SUDAN

South of the Sahara desert, stretching right across Africa from the Atlantic to the Red Sea, is a belt of savannah to which the Arabs gave the name of "Sudan." In the Niger region, in the western half of the Sudan, large, well-organised Negro states were established and flourished during the period called by Europeans the Middle Ages, some of them continuing down to the 19th century. They traded with the Arabs to the north, and Muslim learning and culture was diffused throughout a large part of the area. Timbuktu, on the middle Niger, was an important centre both of Islamism and of commerce.

The map shows only a few of the more outstanding of these kingdoms:—*Ghana* (5th-12th centuries) which lay far to the north of the present Ghana, between the Senegal and the middle Niger; *Mali*, which conquered Ghana, with an empire extending at one time from the Atlantic coast almost as far east as Lake Chad; the *Songhai* kingdom, with its capital at Gao, which was at the height of its power in the 16th century, stretching far north into the Sahara.

When these states declined power moved east to the Hausa kingdoms and Bornu. Later still the kingdoms of Ife and Benin flourished near the mouth of the Niger. By this time, of course, Europeans—Portuguese, British, French, Dutch—were establishing their trading stations along the coast, and the main trade routes were shifting from the Sahara to the Atlantic.

African nationalists today, proud of their history, are reviving the names of these past kingdoms (e.g. Ghana and Mali).

MAP 12

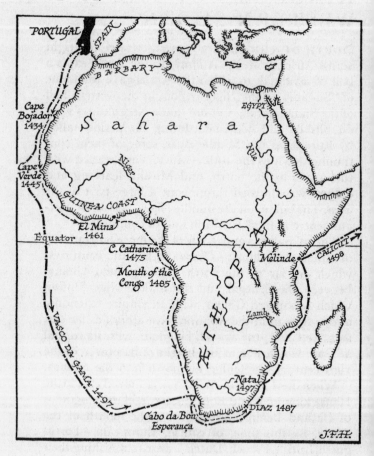

PORTUGAL SPAIN

BARBARY

EGYPT

Sahara

Cape
Bojador
1434

Cape
Verde
1445

Niger

GUINEA COAST

El Mina
1461

Equator

C. Catharine
1475

Mouth of the
Congo 1485

Melinde

CALICUT
1498

ETHIOPIA

VASCO DA GAMA 1497

Zambesi

Natal
1497

Cabo da Boa
Esperança

DIAZ 1487

J.F.H.

42

WESTERN EUROPE
RE-DISCOVERS AFRICA

POMPONIUS MELA, the Roman geographer (A.D. 50) who drew the map inset in No. 8, taught that the earth consisted of continents surrounded by water, and that India therefore could be reached by a sea passage round Africa. Prince Henry of Portugal, called "the Navigator," (1394-1463) believed that P. Mela was right, and sent out expeditions to sail down the African coast. He was also not averse to shipping some of the gold from the Guinea coast, news of which (*via* the Moors) had reached Western Europe. Expedition after expedition sailed. His sailors at first refused to go beyond Cape Bojador, being certain that God would turn them black if they went further. But the following year another ship sailed nearly 400 miles beyond Bojador without dire results.

Prince Henry died in 1463, but the voyages of discovery went on; and at last, in 1487, Bartolomeo Diaz rounded the Cape of Good Hope (having among his crew Columbus's brother). In 1493 Columbus (for Spain) discovered America. Six years later the King of Portugal ordered Vasco da Gama, with three ships, to sail round the Cape and go on to India. For the next three centuries Africa, south of the equator, was for Europeans no more than a coastline, with ports of call, on the way to India.

MAP 13

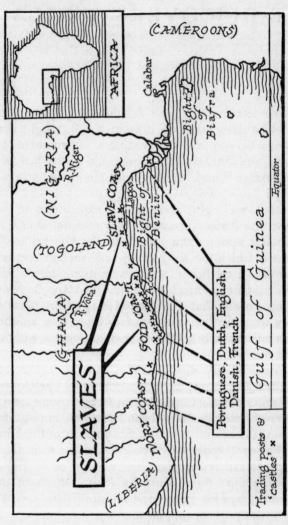

THE SLAVE TRADE

THE 16TH CENTURY opened the Atlantic chapter in European—and world—history. For the next 400 years the European countries facing the Atlantic Ocean were to take the lead in world affairs. The New World, on the western side of the ocean, went by the Pope's orders to Spain (Brazil excepted); Africa and Asia to Portugal. But England and France quickly challenged the Papal dispensation, both in North America and in Africa; and the two sides of the ocean were soon linked in a particularly dreadful way. I quote Norman Leys:[1] "The methods of exploitation followed by the Spaniards in America destroyed by the million the peoples they had conquered. But the exploitation was so profitable that the demand arose for workers who would last longer in slavery on plantations and in mines. That demand, reinforced a little later by Portuguese, French, English and Dutch officials and adventurers, was supplied by West Africa."

The slave trade went on for three centuries. It was perhaps the ghastliest crime (not forgetting Hitler) ever committed against a people.

[1] *Kenya*, p. 22.

MAP 14

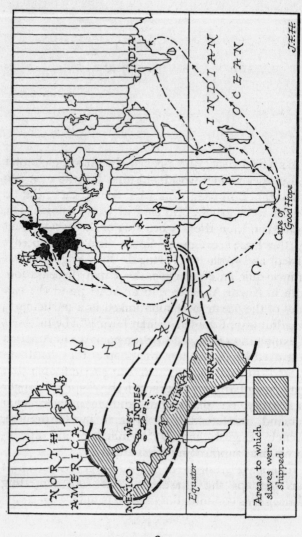

"PIECES OF INDIA"

IN THE REIGN of Charles II this trading prospectus was issued in London:

> "The Spaniards treated with the Royal African Company of England for five thousand whole Pieces of India the Year, for 7 Years to be delivered at some of the Islands . . .
>
> A whole Piece of India was according to the Ages of the Negroes, Male or Female. Those between 15 and 45 were a whole Piece; between 4 and 8 were 2 for 1; between 8 and 15, or above 45, were 3 for 2, and those under 4 were cast in with the Mother.
>
> Such a Trade as this made by an Act of Parliament for 99 Years certain, would much improve all our Western Plantations, and by degrees perhaps find as good Mines in Carolina as in Potosi; 'twou'd increase Seamen and Ships for our use at home and encourage Growths and Manufactures here greatly; 'twill bring us in Gold apace to make Guineas with, and the Goods from the Plantations will fetch us in Silver, besides the Silver gotten for the Blacks. . . ."

At the lowest computation, says Norman Leys, 8 million Africans were sold in America, and at least five times as many persons perished in the slave raids and in the "middle passage"—the voyage across the Atlantic.

MAP 15

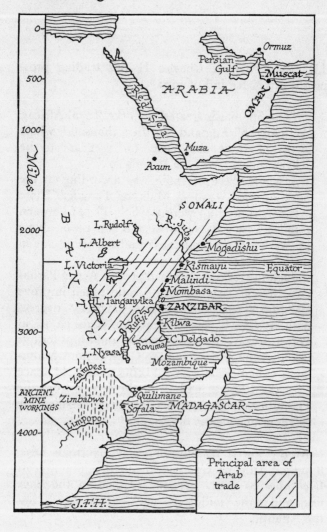

Ormuz

Persian
Gulf

Muscat

ARABIA

OMAN

Red Sea

Muza

Axum

SOMALI

L.Rudolf

R.Juba

Mogadishu

L.Albert

Kismayu

L.Victoria

Equator

B
U
N
Y
O
R
O

Malindi

Mombasa

L.Tanganyika

ZANZIBAR

Rufiji

Kilwa

C.Delgado

Rovuma

L.Nyasa

Mozambique

Zambesi

ANCIENT
MINE
WORKINGS

Zimbabwe
×

Quilimane

Sofala

MADAGASCAR

Limpopo

Miles

0

500

1000

2000

3000

4000

Principal area of
Arab
trade

J.F.H.

THE EAST COAST

OVER ON THE the eastern side of Africa the Arabs had been trading and establishing coastal settlements since the 1st century A.D. According to the *Periplus of the Erythrean Sea*, written by an Egyptian Greek (A.D. 80), East Africa, under the rule of Arabs from Oman, was exporting ivory, rhinoceros horn, and (domestic) slaves. In the 12th century A.D. the Arab historian Edrisi records that the iron of Sofala (the southernmost name on our map) was much in demand by sword-makers in India.

When the Portuguese arrived in the early 16th century they conquered the whole coast from the Limpopo up to the "horn of Africa" (Somaliland). But their hold on the northern part crumbled as their Asiatic empire dwindled, and the Arabs came back into their own everywhere but in the region of Mozambique, which the Portuguese hold to this day (see Map 28). In the middle of the 19th century the Sultan of Oman transferred his "capital" to Zanzibar; and the trade in slaves was still continuing when Livingstone made his journeys of exploration (see next map).

MAP 16

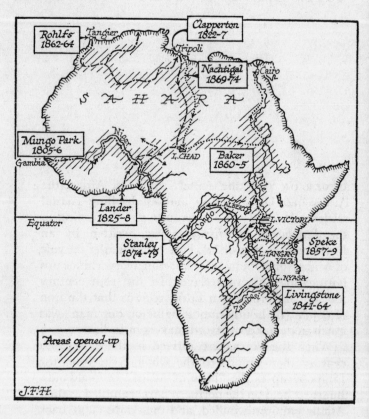

Rohlfs
1862-64

Tangier

Clapperton
1822-7

Tripoli

Nachtigal
1869-74

Cairo

S A H A R A

Niger

L. CHAD

Mungo Park
1805-6

Gambia

Baker
1860-5

Lander
1825-8

Equator

Congo

L. ALBERT

L. VICTORIA

Stanley
1874-79

Speke
1857-9

L. TANGAN-
YIKA

L. NYASA

Livingstone
1841-64

Zambesi

Areas opened-up

J.F.H.

EXPLORERS AND MISSIONARIES

In the last quarter of the 18th century England (or some at least of the English) was beginning to be ashamed of its leading part in the slave trade. The abolitionists were making themselves heard, and a new and more civilised interest in Africa was developing. In 1788 the African Association was formed under the presidency of the scientist, Sir Joseph Banks, and in 1795 it sent out Mungo Park to solve the problem of the Niger. Ten years later Park made a second journey, at Government expense. He established the fact, unknown before, that the Niger flowed eastward. He sailed down the river for nearly two-thirds of its length before he was killed (1806).

From then onwards, for three-quarters of the century, explorers—British, French and German—"opened up" the interior of the Unknown Continent the Sahara, the sources of the Nile, the Congo and Zambesi regions. Some of them were missionaries, some government emissaries. The later explorations, like Stanley's in the Congo region, paved the way for the partition of Africa among the Western European countries.

Some part of Europe's debt to Africa was, and is being, paid by the Christian missions. Until recently they were responsible for whatever educational work was being done; and if many missionaries were narrowly unsympathetic to African culture and ideology, many also were courageous defenders of the African against exploitation of various kinds.

MAP 17

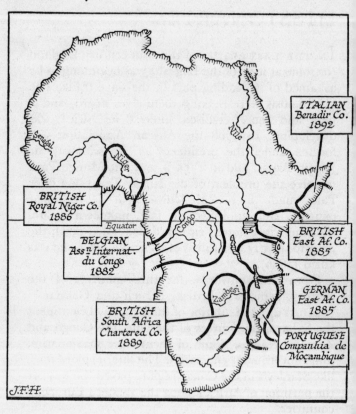

Senegal

Niger

Nile

ITALIAN
Benadir Co.
1892

BRITISH
Royal Niger Co.
1886

Equator

Congo

BELGIAN
Ass.ⁿ Internat.
du Congo
1882

BRITISH
East Af. Co.
1885

GERMAN
East Af. Co.
1885

Zambesi

BRITISH
South Africa
Chartered Co.
1889

PORTUGUESE
Companhia de
Moçambique

J.F.H.

THE CHARTERED
COMPANIES

WE HAVE NOW reached the period of the Great Scramble—turn back to Maps 1 and 2.

Having drawn straight lines[1] in all directions across the map of Africa and parcelled out the continent between them, the European governments gave to Chartered Companies the job (and the profits) of "developing" the hundreds of thousands of square miles of new territory. These Companies were given monopoly rights of exploitation in their respective areas. After a time they were usually bought out, and the territories formally annexed, or placed under "protection." The British operated west, south, and east (see map). King Leopold of the Belgians' Association Internationale du Congo had the centre of the continent. Karl Peters' German East Africa Company, the Portuguese Companhia de Moçambique, and the Italian Benadir Company took areas on the east coast. French trading companies, dating from the 18th century, were still operating from the Senegal region in the north-west.

[1] It should be noted that these straight lines resulted in purely artificial frontiers, which often cut tribes and peoples in two. Now that Africans are claiming the right to govern themselves some re-alignment of frontiers is often essential.

MAP 18

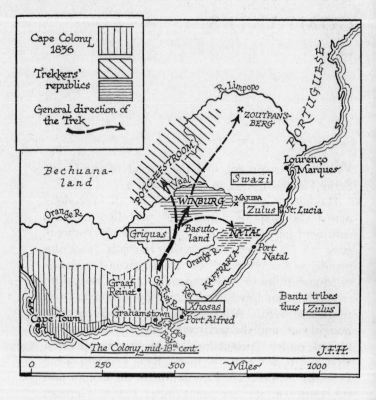

Cape Colony 1836

Trekkers' republics

General direction of the Trek

Bechuana-land

R. Limpopo

×ZOUTPANS-BERG

PORTUGUESE

POTCHEFSTROOM

Orange R.

Vaal

WINBURG

Lourenço Marques

Swazi

MAJUBA ×

Zulus St. Lucia

Griquas

Basuto-land

Orange R.

NATAL

Port Natal

KAFFRARIA

Graaf Reinet

Gt. Fish R.

Kei R.

Xhosas

Bantu tribes thus *Zulus*

Grahamstown

Port Alfred

Cape Town

Algoa Bay

The Colony, mid-18th cent.

J.F.H.

| 0 | 250 | 500 | Miles | 1000 |

54

THE DUTCH TREK NORTH

MORE THAN a century before the British South Africa Chartered Company commenced operations Dutch and British were established in a small colony in the extreme south of the continent, at the Cape. (The Dutchman Van Riebeck had landed with a handful of Dutch and Swedish settlers as far back as 1652, when the Cape was a "cabbage-garden" for the supply of fresh vegetables on the route to India.) The colony changed hands between British and Dutch once or twice during the Napoleonic wars. In 1820 a body of some 5000 English settlers arrived. Fourteen years later, groups of Dutch farmers (Boers), impatient at the more humane British attitude to the natives, trekked north and founded the independent republics of Potchefstroom (later the Transvaal), Winburg (Orange Free State), and Natal. The last-named lasted only ten years, the British annexing it in 1843. The Boer advance was fiercely contested by the Africans—Xhosas, Zulus, Swazis.

In 1877 the two Boer republics were re-annexed to Britain, but only four years later regained their independence after defeating a British force at Majuba Hill.

MAP 19

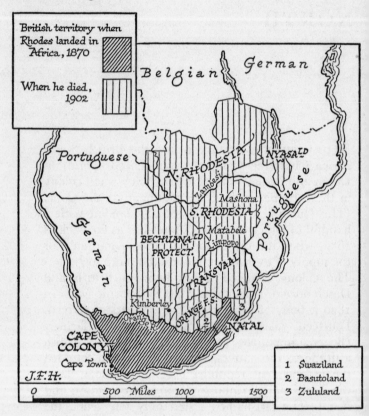

British territory when Rhodes landed in Africa, 1870

When he died, 1902

Belgian

German

Portuguese

N. RHODESIA

NYASA^LD

German

Mashona

Zambesi

S. RHODESIA

BECHUANA^LD PROTECT.

Matabele

Limpopo

TRANSVAAL

Portuguese

Kimberley

ORANGE F.S.

Orange R.

NATAL

CAPE COLONY

Cape Town

J.F.H.

0   500   Miles   1000   1500

1 Swaziland
2 Basutoland
3 Zululand

DIAMONDS AND GOLD

In 1870 a Boer farmer found his children playing with a bright stone. He took it to the nearby town of Kimberley and sold it for £500. A rush of diamond diggers began, and the area was promptly annexed by Britain. Cecil Rhodes' elder brother was among the first prospectors, and Cecil shortly joined him.

In an amazingly short time he was a wealthy man. He did no more digging, concentrating on big business combinations and trusts. De Beers Consolidated Mines had a monopoly of South African diamonds—90% of the world supply. Then gold was discovered on the Rand, in the Transvaal, and Rhodes founded Goldfields of South Africa, Ltd. He went into politics and became Prime Minister of the Cape Colony. His South Africa Chartered Company, after wars with Matabele and Mashonas, secured control of vast areas to the north—Bechuanaland (a protectorate) and the lands north and south of the Zambesi, named after him the Rhodesias.

The map shows the growth of British-controlled territory in South Africa during his lifetime.

MAP 20

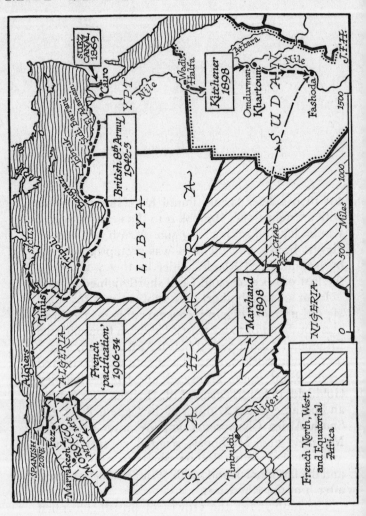

WARS AND "PACIFICA-TIONS" IN THE NORTH

THE MAP COVERS the events of half-a-century in the north of the continent.

In 1885 a religious revolt in the Egyptian Sudan, led by the Mahdi, led to the siege and capture of Khartoum and the killing of General Gordon, head of a British-Egyptian force sent south from British-occupied Egypt (the Suez Canal had been opened in 1869). In 1898 a British-Egyptian army under Kitchener defeated the Khalifa, the Mahdi's successor, at Omdurman, so securing the Sudan for Britain.

A French force under Captain Marchand had been marching eastward through the French Sudan, but reached Fashoda, on the Nile, only to find the Union Jack flying. French Africa was *not* to extend across the continent from west to east.

In 1904 Britain agreed to France having a free hand in Morocco in return for French acquiescence in the British control of Egypt. For nearly 30 years the French were engaged in the "pacification" (i.e. conquest) of Morocco, under the command of the great soldier-administrator, Lyautey.

During the Second World War, after a German-Italian army under Rommel had pushed over the Libyan frontier into Egypt, the British Eighth Army under Montgomery advanced from El Alamein along the thousand miles across Libya to Tunis.

MAP 21

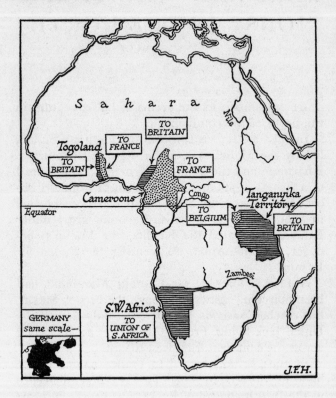

Sahara

TO BRITAIN

TO FRANCE

Togoland

TO BRITAIN

TO FRANCE

Nile

Cameroons

Congo

Equator

TO BELGIUM

Tanganyika Territory

TO BRITAIN

Zambesi

S.W. Africa

TO UNION OF S. AFRICA

GERMANY same scale—

J.F.H.

THE FIRST EUROPEAN
EMPIRE LIQUIDATED

THE PEACE settlement after the First World War
ended the German empire in Africa, the German
colonies being handed over as "mandates" to other
Powers. Togoland and the Cameroons were divided
between Britain and France; German East Africa
was taken over by Britain; as Tanganyika Territory:
a small eastern part of it, Ruanda-Urundi, going to
the Belgian Congo; German South-West Africa to
the Union of South Africa.

After the Second World War the Union of South
Africa declined to make any trusteeship agreement
with the United Nations, and has administered the
territory as a part of the Union. Native lands have
been expropriated for the benefit of white settlers,
and the chiefs of the Herero tribe were prevented
from leaving Africa to present their protest to the
United Nations. Their case was taken up and their
cause pleaded by the Rev. Michael Scott. Seventy
per cent of the *voters* in the territory are Afrikaners,
twenty-two per cent speak German, and the
remainder English.

61

MAP 22

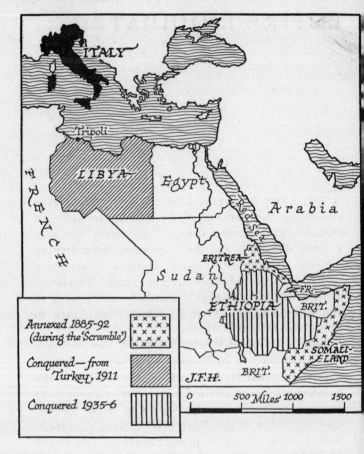

ITALY

Tripoli

LIBYA

Egypt

FRENCH

Red Sea

Arabia

ERITREA

Sudan

ETHIOPIA

FR.

BRIT.

SOMALILAND

BRIT.

J.F.H.

Annexed 1885-92
(during the 'Scramble')

Conquered—from
Turkey, 1911

Conquered 1935-6

0   500 *Miles* 1000   1500

—AND THE SECOND

Italy's empire in Africa consisted of Eritrea and Somaliland, north and south-east respectively of Ethiopia (Abyssinia); and Libya, conquered from Turkey in 1911-12. An Italian invasion of Abyssinia in 1896 came to a disastrous conclusion at Adowa. Mussolini avenged this defeat by the successful war of 1935. But at the end of the Second World War Ethiopia regained its independence, and Eritrea became an autonomous province under Ethiopian suzerainty. Italian Somaliland became Somalia, a trusteeship territory under Italian administration until December, 1960, when it will become an independent sovereign state—probably linked with British Somaliland.

Libya became independent in 1951.

PART II

TODAY

MAP 23

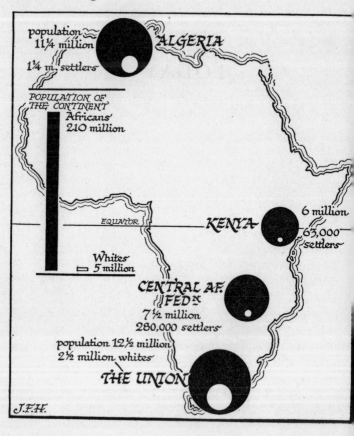

population
1¼ million

1¼ m. settlers

ALGERIA

POPULATION OF
THE CONTINENT
Africans'
210 million

EQUATOR

KENYA

6 million

63,000
settlers

Whites
5 million

CENTRAL AF.
FED^N
7½ million
280,000 settlers

population 12½ million
2½ million whites

THE UNION

J.F.H.

THE TROUBLE SPOTS

THE FOUR BLACK blots—one should rather say white blots—on the map of Africa, the spots which keep Africa on the front page of the newspapers, are the four areas where there has been considerable white settlement.

The French connection with ALGERIA began in 1830, when a French fleet bombarded and occupied Algiers, the capital city of a sultanate notorious for piracy. For forty years after that there were fierce revolts by the Arabs, but settlement (by Italians as well as French) in the fertile coast lands steadily increased.

Dutch and British settlement in the UNION OF SOUTH AFRICA has already been mentioned (Map 18).

In KENYA and the RHODESIAS (Central African Federation) white settlement began only in the present century. The highlands of Kenya, though situated so near the equator, have a climate suited to Europeans, and the same is true of Central Africa. In both these territories, as in the Union, administration, the professions, and all skilled labour are a virtual monopoly of the whites, Africans doing the menial and manual work.

MAP 24

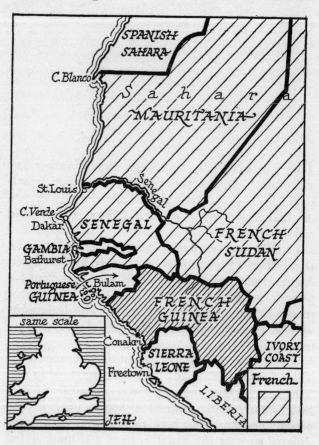

WEST COAST
BEGINNINGS

THE RELATIVELY small colonies on the west coast—British, French, Portuguese, Spanish—mostly date from the days before the Great Scramble.

SPANISH Sahara (*Rio de Oro*) is mainly desert, with a sparse population of nomad Arabs.

FRANCE has *Senegal* (with Dakar, the capital of all French West Africa) and *Mauritania*. *Guinea* declared for independence in the referendum of 1958.

PORTUGUESE *Guinea* was founded 500 years ago, in the days when Prince Henry's seamen made their first daring voyages down the African coast.

The small BRITISH colony of the *Gambia* is likely, so it is said, to be absorbed by French Senegal soon. To judge from the map this would be sensible. *Sierra Leone* was originally (end of 18th century) an asylum for Africans rescued from slave-ships and destitute negroes from England. (Between 1810 and 1864 the Royal Navy rescued 150,000 men and women from the slavers.)

For LIBERIA see Map 38. 37

MAP 25

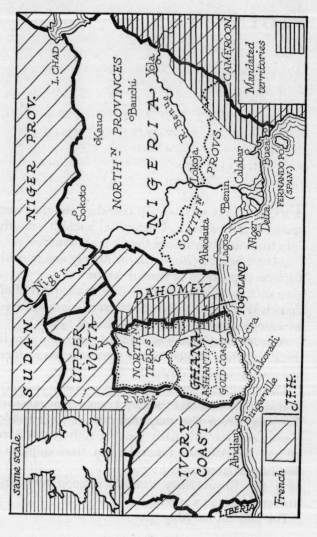

WEST COAST *(continued)*

"ROUND THE corner," along the Guinea Coast, are some of the most prosperous and densely populated areas in all Africa. Between a quarter and a third of the total population of the continent lives in this region. Slaves are no longer a primary commodity, but the gold, cocoa, palm-oil and groundnuts produced here put Africa definitely on the world's economic map.

This is the region for long known as the White Man's Grave, and though modern medical science has made life here no longer impossible for Europeans, there is no settler problem and no alienated land. (An African has suggested that a statue of the mosquito should be erected, with some such inscription as "He saved us from the Whites.") Peasant proprietors and co-operatives are responsible for practically all production.

Ghana[1] (about the size of Great Britain and Northern Ireland) achieved independence in 1957.

Nigeria[1] will attain the same status in 1960. The Trust territory of *East Togoland* was joined to Ghana in 1956. The *Northern Cameroons* is to become part of Northern Nigeria; the people of the *Southern Cameroons* have yet to decide whether they will join Nigeria or the French Cameroons.

[1] And see Map 38.

71

MAP 26

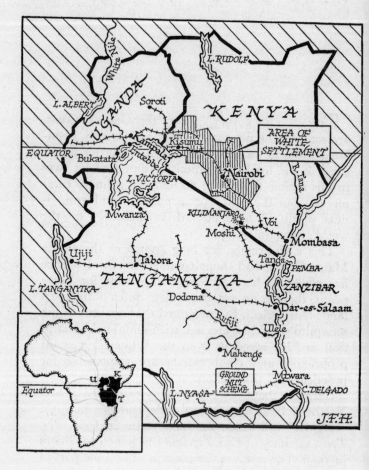

EAST COAST (BRITISH)

KENYA, *Uganda*, *Tanganyika* and *Zanzibar*, the
four British-controlled territories in East Africa, form
an area nearly a quarter the size of the U.S.A. Their
joint population is 21 millions (a quarter of the
U.S.A.'s population=40 millions.) The coast towns
(see Map 15) were under Arab dominance for centuries. Inland is the great lake region—Lake Victoria
is the third largest inland water in the world.

The highlands of *Kenya* were opened and reserved
to white settlement just before the First World War.
Their fertility—and the suitability of the climate—
had been realised during the construction of the
Uganda railway from the coast to Kampala. The
Africans were accordingly crowded into reserves
(Kikuyu reserve, density 283 per square mile, Kavi-
rondo 145). African "unrest" reached a climax in
the Mau Mau rebellion in 1952-3.

Zanzibar came under British protection soon
after the British East Africa Co. was formed (see
Map 17). According to an official historian the
Sultan realised "his long-cherished wish to defend
his rights from further encroachment by granting the
concession to the Company." As Leonard Woolf has
commented:[1] "The phenomenon of rulers with
'long cherished wishes' to give away their territory is
so remarkable that investigation is desirable."

Tanganyika, formerly German East Africa,
although it has some thousands of white settlers and
a large body of Asiatics, has so far had a far more
civilised Native Policy than its neighbours (Kenya to
the north and the Central African Federation to the
southwest).

[1] *Empire and Commerce in Africa.*

MAP 27

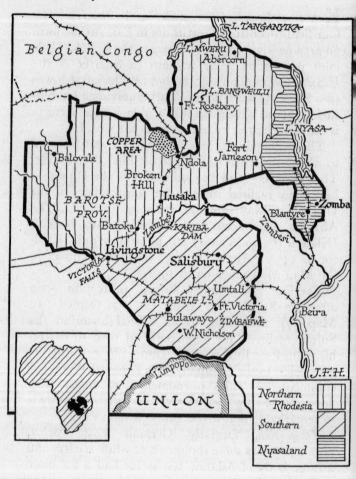

Belgian Congo

L. TANGANYKA
L. MWERU
Abercorn
L. BANGWEULU
Ft. Rosebery
L. NYASA
COPPER AREA
Balovale
Ndola
Fort Jameson
Broken Hill
Lusaka
BAROTSE PROV.
Batoka
Zambesi
Zomba
Blantyre
KARIBA DAM
Zambesi
Livingstone
VICTORIA FALLS
Salisbury
Umtali
MATABELE L^D.
Ft. Victoria
Beira
Bulawayo
ZIMBABWE
W. Nicholson
Limpopo
UNION

J.F.H.

Northern Rhodesia
Southern
Nyasaland

FROM RHODES TO WELENSKY

THE Central African Federation as we have seen (Map 19) is a British heritage from the era of Cecil Rhodes—and, since it includes Nyasaland, from the days of a very different man, David Livingstone. *Nyasaland*, though by far the smallest in area of the three territories, has a larger population than either of the *two Rhodesias*.

The native policy of the C.A.F. is allegedly based on "partnership"; but it is clearly a partnership of first- and second-class citizens. Cecil Rhodes' declaration, late in his life, for *"equal rights for all civilised men, black or white"* has been circumvented by civilisation "tests" which give limited rights to a small minority of black men only.

Nyasaland asked for British protection in 1891, largely as a result of missionary effort by the Church of Scotland. *Matabeleland* was occupied after the Matabele War in 1893, and *Southern Rhodesia* was constituted in 1898. It was granted limited self-government in 1923, after white settlement had already reached considerable figures. Federation of the three areas was inaugurated in 1953, despite emphatic opposition by the Africans of Nyasaland.

The copper field of *Northern Rhodesia* is the third largest in the world.

MAP 28

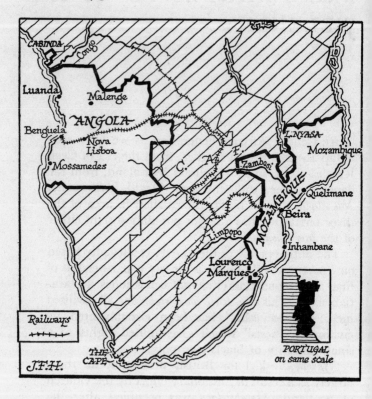

CABINDA

Congo

Luanda •Malenge

ANGOLA

Benguela •Nova Lisboa

•Mossamedes

C. A. F.

L. NYASA

Mozambique

•Zambesi

MOZAMBIQUE

•Quelimane

•Beira

Limpopo

•Inhambane

Lourenço Marques•

Railways

THE CAPE

J.F.H.

PORTUGAL
on same scale

76

PORTUGAL IN AFRICA

THE NOT inconsiderable remains of Portugal's once vast overseas empire, *Angola* and *Mozambique*, on the west and east coast of Africa respectively, are probably the most backward areas of the whole continent; backward, that is, judged by civilised standards—economically they are undoubtedly paying propositions.

The Benguela railway, running east across Angola, links up with the central Cape-Congo line, from which, in Southern Rhodesia, a line runs to Beira, in Mozambique, thus completing the only through west-east railway across Africa. Beira is an entrepôt port for the Rhodesias, the Belgian Congo, and Nyasaland; while Lourenço Marques, further south, is guaranteed 50 to 55% of traffic from the Rand (Transvaal) in return for recruiting labour for the Rand mines.

Native policy is alleged to aim at "spiritual assimilation"; that is, of denying all political rights to Africans who have not "acquired a European outlook." Such Africans form, of course, the vast majority; and being merely "aborigines" are liable, on occasion, to forced labour.

MAP 29

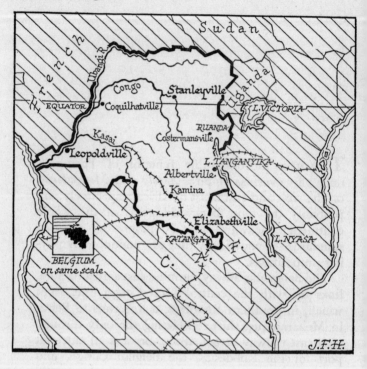

KING LEOPOLD'S
CRUSADE

In 1876 King Leopold II of the Belgians summoned a "geographic conference" at Brussels, and made a speech in which he said—"To open to civilisation the only area where it has not yet penetrated, to pierce the darkness which envelops whole populations, is a crusade . . . a crusade worthy of this century of progress." Two years later H. M. Stanley returned from his journey down the Congo, and King Leopold, having in the meantime formed some Belgian business men into a "Committee for the Study of the Upper Congo," sent Stanley back to Africa to found "stations" on the river and to make treaties with native chiefs. A year or two later, in 1885, the Congo Free State was inaugurated, with Leopold as its sovereign. Concessionaire companies got busy—one of them made in six years a net profit of over 3 million dollars on a paid-up capital of 45,000.[1]

The Congo got on to the front pages again a few years later when Roger Casement's investigations found that the inhabitants were being treated "with inconceivable brutality," and E. D. Morel, in *Red Rubber*, gave the facts to the world.

In 1908 the "Free State" became a Belgian colony, and a "paternalist" native policy was instituted. But the U.N. had to condemn Belgium for refusing Africans any political voice, and recent "unrest" has compelled the Belgian Government to speed up reforms and promise—ultimately, of course—independence.

[1] P. T. Moon, *Imperialism and World Politics*, p. 87.

MAP 30

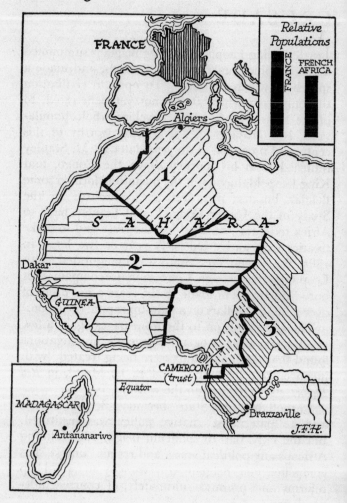

FRANCE

Relative
Populations

FRANCE

FRENCH
AFRICA

Algiers

1

S A H A R A

Dakar

2

GUINEA

3

CAMEROON
(trust)

Congo

Brazzaville

J.F.H.

Equator

MADAGASCAR

Antananarivo

FRENCH AFRICA

FRENCH AFRICA (exclusive of Madagascar) covers
a vast area of about 4 million square miles—nearly
twice as large as the U.S.A., with less than a quarter
of the U.S.A.'s population.

This map shows the three main zones: (1) *French
North Africa*, now, after the winning of independence
by Morocco and Tunisia, reduced to Algeria.
(2) *French West Africa*, with its administrative centre
at Dakar (for the territories comprised see next map).
Guinea, in the referendum in 1958, alone voted for
complete independence. (3) *French Equatorial Africa*,
extending south of the equator to the Congo.

All these territories have been linked pretty
closely to France. J. H. Huizinga points out (*African
Affairs*, January, 1959) that "the French tax-payer
in the last ten years has provided about five times
more for the French African territories than the
British tax-payer has provided for British Africa
which has twice the population"; a fact which had
doubtless something to do with the decision of most
of the territories to remain within the French Community. Indeed, Dr. Houphouet-Birgny, leader of
the largest nationalist movement in French Africa,
has said: "If we had been colonised by the English,
no doubt we too would have opted for independence."

The island of *Madagascar* (population nearly
5 millions, 50,000 Europeans) has been French—
after a bombardment of the capital—since 1896. A
revolt in 1947 cost some thousands of lives. It is now an
autonomous republic, within the French Community.

MAP 31

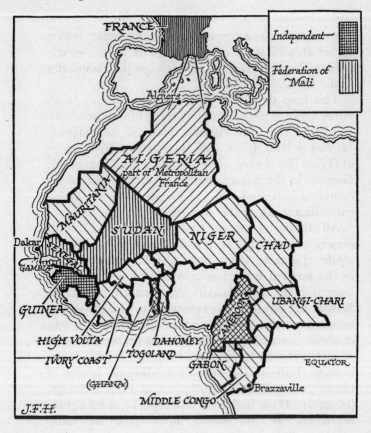

FRANCE

Independent

Federation of
Mali

Algiers

ALGERIA
part of Metropolitan
France

MAURITANIA

SUDAN

NIGER

CHAD

Dakar

GAMBIA

GUINEA

UBANGI-CHARI

HIGH VOLTA

DAHOMEY

CAMEROON

IVORY COAST

TOGOLAND

(GHANA)

GABON

EQUATOR

MIDDLE CONGO

Brazzaville

J.F.H.

FRENCH AFRICA *(continued)*

GUINEA, THE ONLY one of the French territories to declare for sovereign independence in the
1958 Referendum, has since decided on a close union
with Ghana. (A not inconsiderable obstacle to this
union is that the prime ministers of the two states can
only talk through an interpreter. They have no
common African language; President Touré speaks
only French, Dr. Nkrumah only English.) The other
territories (Algeria excepted) are now autonomous
republics within the French Community.

Two important questions have still to be answered.
(1) Will these republics all remain separate or will
they federate—in one body, or in groups of two or
three? *Senegal* and *Sudan* have already formed the
Federation of Mali. The four equatorial territories,
Chad, *Ubangi-Chari*, *Gabon* and the *Middle Congo* have
banded together in a customs and economic union.
(2) Will the present right-wing French National
Assembly really acquiesce in treating these ex-
colonies as equals in the French Community?

Togoland and the *Cameroons*, both trust territories,
are to become independent next year.

MAP 32

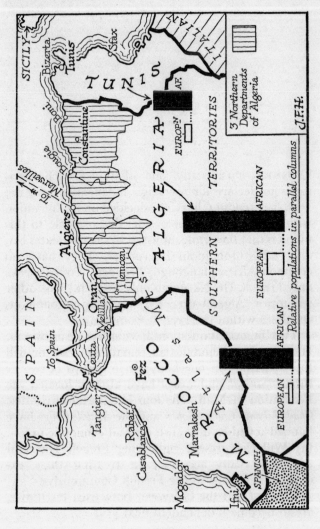

SICILY

Bizerta
Tunis
Sfax

TUNIS

Bône

Bougie

Constantine

To Marseilles

Algiers

SPAIN

To Spain

Oran
Melilla
Tlemcen
Ceuta

MTS.

Fez

Tangier

Rabat
Casablanca

Marrakesh

Mogador

Ifni

SPANISH

MOROCCO

ATLAS

ALGERIA

AF.

EUROP'N

SOUTHERN   TERRITORIES

AFRICAN

EUROPEAN

AFRICAN

EUROPEAN

Relative populations in parallel columns

3 Northern
Departments
of Algeria

J.F.H.

ITALIAN

THE ARABS MAKE WAR

AT THE All-Africa Congress in Accra, December,
1958, the Algerian delegation moved and carried an
amendment to the platform resolution urging the
attainment of independence by peaceful, constitutional methods. Where violence is used against a
nationalist movement, said the Algerians, Africans
must give their support to violent resistance.

For more than four years the bloody struggle has
gone on in *Algeria*; and *Morocco* and *Tunis*, which
won their independence from France in 1956, are
torn between sympathy for their Algerian brethren
and their desperate need to retain their economic
links with France. In Tunisia, it is estimated a
tenth of the population is unemployed. Yet Tunis
cannot avoid establishing supply depots for the
Algerian rebels along its frontiers—which does not
increase French friendship. In Morocco, King
Mohammed V faces leftist nationalist movements
anxious to end his pro-Western policies, and to turn
the U.S. out of its Moroccan naval and air bases.

Meantime the French settlers of Algeria set their
faces against any concessions by De Gaulle to the
"rebels," preferring, it would seem, to bring down
the Fifth Republic.

MAP 33

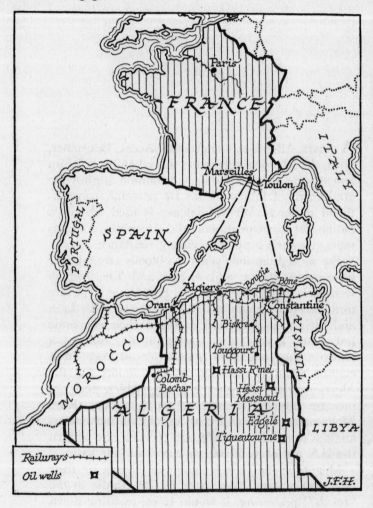

Railways +++++
Oil wells ⊠

Paris

FRANCE

ITALY

Marseilles
Toulon

SPAIN

PORTUGAL

Algiers
Bougie
Bône
Oran
Constantine

MOROCCO

Biskra

Touggourt

TUNISIA

Hassi R'mel

Colomb-
Bechar

Hassi
Messaoud

ALGERIA

Edgelé

LIBYA

Tiguentourine

J.F.H.

ALGERIA—EUROPEAN OR AFRICAN?

ALGERIA WAS THE first of the North African countries to be occupied by the French (1842), but it was many years before Arab resistance was over-come. "This resistance," Edward Atiyah points out,[1] "was the first reaction (a century ago) of the western Arab world to European imperialism." It is a grim coincidence that French Resistance to the German occupation of France stood up heroically to torture; and that Arab Resistance to the French occupation of Algeria has faced the same treatment.

The French, of course, now insist that Algeria is an integral part of metropolitan France; which means that the Arabs, in a large majority in Algeria, would be a permanent minority in France-cum-Algeria.

The discovery of oil in the Sahara has naturally not made France any more anxious to hand over Algeria to the Algerians. The four-year war in Algeria has been as a matter of fact the biggest overseas military effort ever made by France. A Five Year Plan (economic and political) for Algeria, the "Constantine Programme," was announced by General de Gaulle in October, 1958.

[1] *The Arabs*, p. 139.

MAP 34

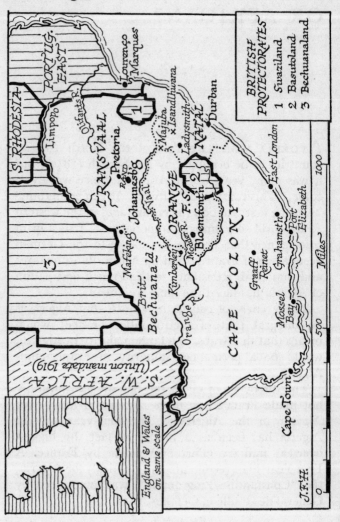

BRITISH PROTECTORATES
1 Swaziland
2 Basutoland
3 Bechuanaland

S. RHODESIA

PORTUG. EAST

Limpopo R.

Olifants R.

Lourenço Marques

TRANSVAAL

Pretoria

Rand

Johannesburg

Mafeking

Brit. Bechuana ld.

3

Vaal R.

Kimberley

Modder R.

ORANGE F.S.

Bloemfontein 2

Majuba
x Isandhlwana

Ladysmith

NATAL

Durban

East London

CAPE COLONY

Orange R.

Graaff Reinet

Grahamstn

Port Elizabeth

Mossel Bay

S.W. AFRICA
(Union mandate 1919)

Cape Town

England & Wales
on same scale

J.F.H.

0   500   1000
Miles

88

THE HOME OF APARTHEID

THE BRITISH Liberal Government's decision (1909) to hand South Africa back to the Boers was hailed as a piece of generous and constructive statesmanship towards a defeated enemy. But, says Leonard Barnes,[1] "in doing a good turn to the Boers that Government did a very bad one to the much more numerous but defenceless natives. . . . As it happened there was a native population three times as large as Boers and Britons put together. . . . By its gesture of magnaminity towards the Boers, the Liberal Government virtually washed its hands of this [native] difficulty."

The South African Nationalist Party (in power since 1948) stands for the old Boer doctrine of White Supremacy. Its native policy is expressed in one word—*Apartheid*: segregation of blacks from whites, with all power, prestige, profit and political rights to the latter. It is a crazy doctrine, of course, as well as an immoral and un-Christian one—South Africa cannot develop as a modern industrial state without African labour. Whether there can be any change in the existing situation without violent revolution remains to be seen.

The Union would like to absorb the three British Protectorates, two of them, *Swaziland* and *Basutoland*, within its borders. So far, no British Government has stooped so low as to consider handing them over.

[1] *The New Boer War.*

MAP 35

Nationalist Party

United Party

Doubtful

S. RHODESIA

Bechuanaland Protect.

S.W. AFRICA

TRANSVAAL

Pretoria

Mafeking

Johannesb'g

Vereeniging

1

Kimberley

ORANGE F.S.

2

NATAL

Durban

C A P E

1 – Swaziland
2 – Basutoland

East London

Cape Town

Port Elizabeth

J.F.H.

THE POLITICS OF INEQUALITY

THE STRENGTH AND extent of the Nationalist
Party in the Union of South Africa is illustrated by
this map (copied, by permission, from *The Politics of
Inequality*, by Gwen M. Carter). It is based on the
results of the General Election of April, 1953. The
United Party (the official Opposition) is practically
confined, it will be noted, to the eastern end of the
Cape Province and the old British colony of Natal,
with smaller areas near Cape Town and Johannesburg.

The United Party does not oppose Apartheid—
only some of the means used or proposed for carrying
it into effect.

MAP 36

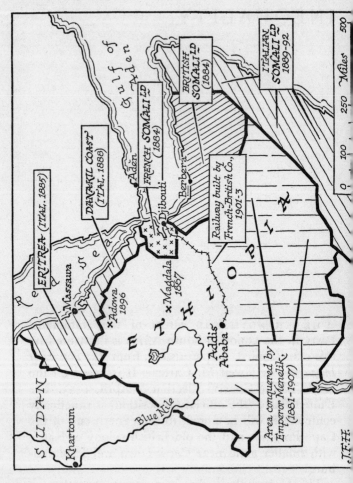

ERITREA (ITAL. 1885)

DANAKIL COAST (ITAL. 1888)

FRENCH SOMALI LD (1884)

BRITISH SOMALI LD (1884)

ITALIAN SOMALI LD 1889-92

Railway built by French-British Co., 1901-3

Area conquered by Emperor Menelik (1881-1907)

Gulf of Aden

Aden

Djibouti

Berbera

×Adowa 1896

×Magdala 1867

Addis Ababa

Massawa

ETHIOPIA

SUDAN

Khartoum

Blue Nile

Red Sea

0   100   250   500 Miles

J.F.H.

MOUNTAIN KINGDOM

Except for the six years of the Italian occupation (1935-41) *Ethiopia* (Abyssinia) has kept its independence throughout the centuries of recorded African history.

It was invaded by the British, and its ruler defeated at Magdala, in 1867; and by the Italians, whom it heavily defeated at Adowa, in 1896. The same two Powers, *plus* France, snatched the coastlands all round it during the Great Scramble. Its ruler at this time, the Emperor Menelik, did some conquering on his own account, annexing large areas to the south of his original territory. It was in the latter years of his reign that a railway was built, linking his capital, Addis Ababa, to the coast at the French port of Djibouti.

By U.N. resolution the former Italian colony of *Eritrea* was federated (1952) with Ethiopia, which thus at last gained direct access to the sea.

MAP 37

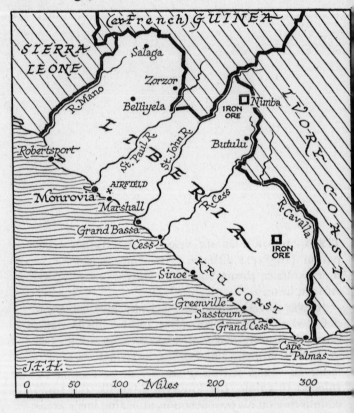

(exFrench) GUINEA

SIERRA LEONE

Salaga

Zorzor

R.Mano

Belliyela

Numba
IRON ORE

IVORY COAST

L I B E R I A

Robertsport

St.Paul R.

St.John R.

Butulu

AIRFIELD
✕
Monrovia

Marshall

R.Cess

R.Cavalla

IRON ORE

Grand Bassa

Cess

Sinoe

KRU COAST

Greenville

Sasstown

Grand Cess

Cape Palmas

J.F.H.

| 0 | 50 | 100 | Miles | 200 | | 300 |

U.S.-ADOPTED

One small independent African state has been in existence on the West Coast for over a century—*Liberia*. The American Government was finding the numbers of freed slaves an embarrassment, so a piece of territory adjoining Sierra Leone (also a home for freed slaves) was purchased, and the first batch of American negroes settled there, in 1822. The original area has been considerably increased since, and the tribes of the interior brought under the rule of their "Europeanised" brethren on the coast. Large road-building schemes have recently been inaugurated. So far, the Liberian Government has shown no eagerness to assist in the realisation of Pan-African ideals, or even to enter into any kind of closer union with such new states as Ghana or Guinea.

The (American) Firestone Company and the Goodrich Co. have extensive rubber plantations, and American, German, and Swedish-American companies are developing big iron-ore projects. The U.S. dollar is the medium of exchange.

MAP 38

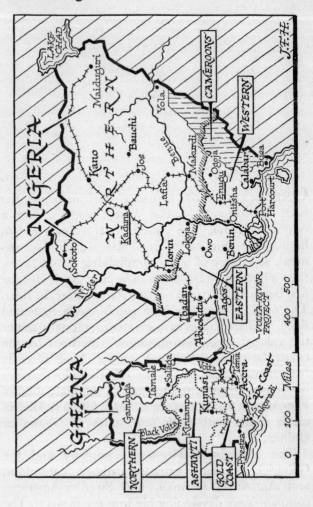

NEW STATES

In March, 1957, the colony of the Gold Coast became the first British African territory to become an independent state. It called itself *Ghana*, from the ancient Negro Kingdom of that name (see Map 11). It is governed by the Convention People's Party, which first won power in the Colony in 1950, its leader then and now being Dr. Kwame Nkrumah. Its peoples speak various African languages, but the official language (and the language of its Parliament) is English. It exports cocoa (70% of the total value of exports), gold, bauxite, timber and diamonds, through two deep-water ports, Takoradi and Tema. The Volta River Project, to be administered on the lines of the T.V.A. in the United States, would generate electricity, supply water for irrigation, and exploit the large deposits of bauxite and aluminium.

In 1960 the Federation of *Nigeria* also becomes independent. Its three regions—*Northern, Western* and *Eastern* (capitals, Kaduna, Ibadan and Enugu)—each have their own governments, and the former trust territory of the *Cameroons* also. Agriculture produces 90% of Nigeria's exports and occupies 80% of its working population. But it also exports 5% of the world's tin, and oilfields in Eastern Nigeria, with a pipeline to Port Harcourt, are now being developed. After Egypt, Nigeria (see Map 42) is the area of densest population in Africa. Here, too, English is the official language.

MAP 39

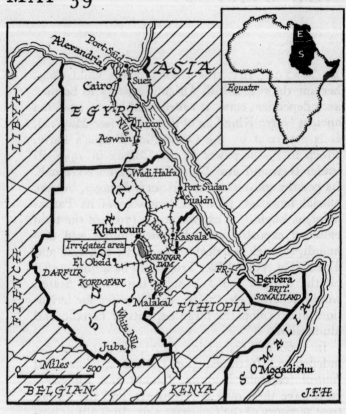

THE COUNTRIES OF
THE NILE

Egypt, under British administration from 1882
(from 1914 to 1922 it was a British Protectorate)
became independent in 1936, but Britain still kept
the right to maintain a garrison on the Suez Canal.
In 1956, on the accession to the Presidency of
Colonel Gamal Nasser, that garrison was withdrawn.
Later that year, after Nasser had without warning
nationalised the Canal, Britain, France and Israel
invaded Egypt, but in deference to world opinion
ceased hostilities in a few days. The "Suez Incident"
undoubtedly strengthened Colonel Nasser's position
as leader of the Arab world against the West.

The Sudan, before it attained full independence in
1956 had been an Anglo-Egyptian Condominium
since 1899. Colonel Nasser's attempts to persuade it
to accept some form of closer union with Egypt have
so far failed. The key fact in Sudanese politics is the
division of the country between an Arab-speaking
Moslem north and a non-Moslem Negro south. The
great achievement of British rule was the construction of the Sennar and Jebel Aulia dams, and the
establishment of the highly successful co-operative
cotton-growing enterprise—the Gezira Scheme;
described in a Fabian pamphlet some years ago as
"one of the most interesting social, political and
economic experiments outside the Soviet Union,"
representing "a very advanced stage of socialised
farming."

MAP 40

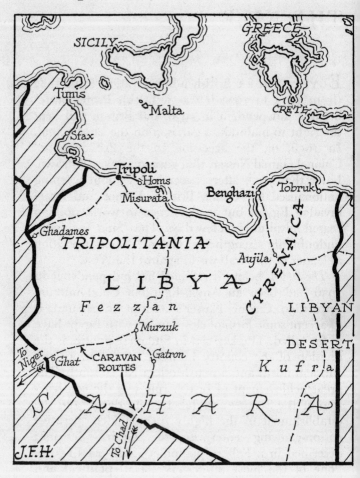

DESERT COUNTRY

LIBYA, WITH AN area larger than France, Italy, Britain, Spain and Germany combined, has a population of a little over a million. The country is mainly rock and sand desert, the few towns lying along the fertile coast strip. From the 16th century Libya was under Turkish rule, until, a couple of years before the First World War, Italy seized it, and proceeded to put a good deal of road construction in hand. There was a certain amount of Italian settlement, and an Italian minority still remains in Tripolitania. Libya is now a constitutional monarchy under King Idris I, the head of the Senussi, the Arab sect most fiercely and irreconcilably hostile to the Italians.

Oil has been found in Algeria, just west of the Libyan frontier (see Map 47); a discovery of it on the Libyan side would obviously make a revolutionary change in the country's economic position.

MAP 41

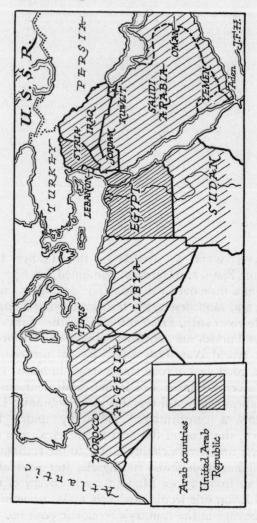

Arab countries

United Arab Republic

COLONEL NASSER'S VISION

MODERN POLITICAL and economic develop-
ment ignores the academic division of the world into
continents. France wishes to make Algeria part of
Europe. Colonel Nasser, as leader of the Arab world,
would like the whole of North Africa to be in close
union with Western Asia (i.e. with the Middle East)
an area extending from the Atlantic to the Persian
Gulf. The internal politics of the Arab countries, as
has been obvious in Iraq since the revolution of
1958, are very largely concerned with the struggle
between pro-Nasser and anti-Nasser elements. The
monarchies of Morocco, Libya and Saudi Arabia
tend to stand aloof from him, and so far only one of
the Arab republics, Syria, has accepted closer union
with Egypt. An Egyptian delegation took part in the
All-Africa Conference in December, 1958; and the
Afro-Asian People's Solidarity Council, on which
forty African and Asian peoples are represented, has
as one of its main aims "active help to the freedom
movements in the still dependent countries of Africa."

PART III

TOMORROW

MAP 42

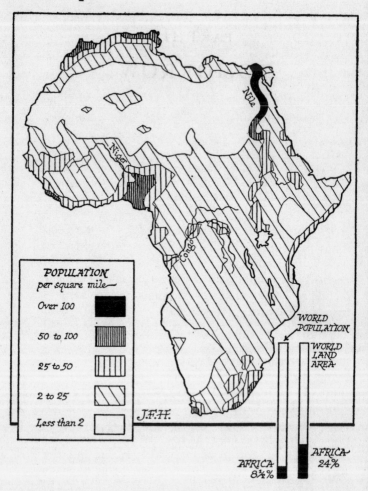

POPULATION
per square mile —

Over 100

50 to 100

25 to 50

2 to 25

Less than 2

Nile

Niger

Congo

J.F.H.

WORLD
POPULATION

WORLD
LAND
AREA

AFRICA
8½%

AFRICA
24%

MORE SETTLERS
NEEDED?

THE ANSWER IS emphatically "Yes." It is a good
many years now since Norman Leys, after years of
service in Kenya, urged that what Africa most
needed was numbers of *lay* missionaries—scientists,
technical experts, skilled workmen of all kinds—
men and women prepared to live and work with
Africans on equal terms, to put their knowledge and
skill at the Africans' disposal, to *help* (not "direct")
in the colossal task of bringing African standards of
living up to the level of Europe's; Europeans, in
short, like Dr. Albert Schweitzer and Mr. Guy
Clutton-Brock. Europeans owe that debt to Africans.
And Africa—leaving out the great deserts—is under-
populated. Three times the size of Europe it has less
than a third of Europe's population. As another
Kenya doctor[1] has written: "Only by breaking away
from the evil heritage of the past, and by a *change of
direction by men of all races*, can Africa find salvation."

[1] C. J. Wilson, *Before the White Man in Kenya.*

MAP 43

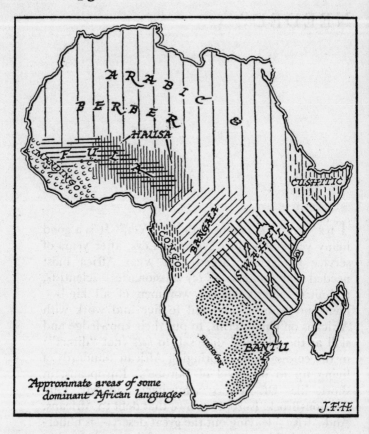

Approximate areas of some
dominant African languages

J.F.H.

THE PROBLEM OF
LANGUAGE

THIS IS A GROSSLY over-simplified map, showing the broad distribution of some main language-
groups in Africa. These should be broken down into
scores of languages, most of them, of course, without
any written alphabet as yet. Anthropologists in all
parts of the continent are at work on this problem.

For practical purposes—commerce, education,
administration—the languages of present-day Africa
are Arabic, English, French, Swahili and Afrikaans.
As we have seen, the new parliaments of Ghana and
Nigeria carry on their debates in English; and those
of the French republics in French. Swahili, the
lingua franca of the East Coast, is a mixture of Arabic
and Bantu. Afrikaans is confined to the Union of
South Africa.

Like nationalists everywhere (e.g. in Ireland and
Wales) African nationalists wish to preserve their
languages. But if education, for instance, had to
await the translation of essential textbooks into every
African language the march of progress would be
slowed down to a crawl. English and French will
inevitably be used more and more. (Soviet broad-
casts to Africa are in these two languages.)

MAP 44

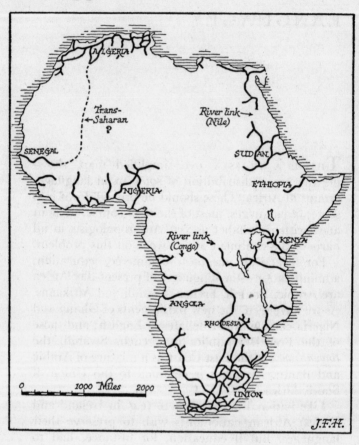

SENEGAL

ALGERIA

Trans-
←Saharan
?

River link
(Nile)

SUDAN

ETHIOPIA

NIGERIA

River link
(Congo)

KENYA

ANGOLA

RHODESIA

UNION

0   1000 Miles   2000

J.F.H.

THE PROBLEM OF TRANSPORT

AFRICA, IT IS scarcely surprising to learn, has fewer miles of railroad than any other continent. Only in the north (Morocco, Algeria, Tunis) and in the extreme south (the Union) is there anything like a developed network, with rather less elaborate systems in the other two "settler" areas, Kenya and Rhodesia. Cecil Rhodes' dream of a Cape-to-Cairo line was never realised. Such as they are, the railways, as is obvious from the map, have been constructed to feed particular ports.

All-weather roads may well play a bigger part than railways in the Africa of the future. Public work departments and laboratories in various territories are today studying road materials, soil mechanics, etc.

Air-lines, of course, now link the various parts of the continent. There must be many Africans to whom an aeroplane is a familiar sight who have never seen a railway train.

The Colonial Development Corporation, inaugurated by the 1945-50 Labour Government, has played an important part in various schemes of economic development in the British territories—transport, mining, agriculture, etc.

MAP 45

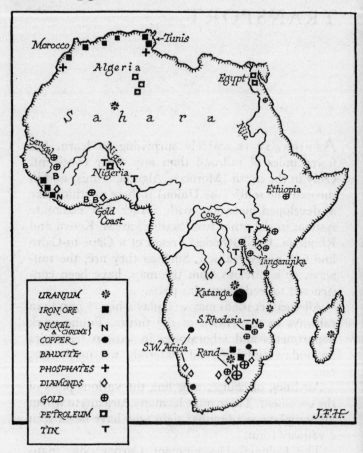

Morocco
←Tunis
Algeria
Egypt
Sahara
Nile
Senegal
Niger
Nigeria
Gold
Coast
Ethiopia
Congo
Tanganyika
Katanga
S. Rhodesia
S.W. Africa
Rand
J.F.H.

URANIUM
IRON ORE
NICKEL
& CHROME }
COPPER
BAUXITE
PHOSPHATES
DIAMONDS
GOLD
PETROLEUM
TIN

MINERAL WEALTH

Gold was a major objective of the first European traders to West Africa, and it is still mined in Ghana (the Gold Coast). But the richest goldfields were only discovered in the late 19th century, on the Rand, in the Transvaal (and they were a primary cause of the Boer War). There is gold also in Kenya, Tanganyika, and Rhodesia. Kimberley was once the most important diamond field, but the largest fields now are in the Belgian Congo and in South-West Africa (held by the Union). The other most important metal area in Africa is the Katanga copper belt, divided between the Congo and N. Rhodesia.

In all these mining centres the labour is African, and a major problem results from the male populations of whole areas leaving their village to work, on two-or-three-year contracts, in the mines; doubly a problem because not only are the villages denuded of active workers, but the miners are brought into contact with "civilisation" at its rawest and crudest.

Great reserves of bauxite in Ghana and Guinea, and of iron ore in Mauritania and Liberia, have as yet hardly been worked.

MAP 46

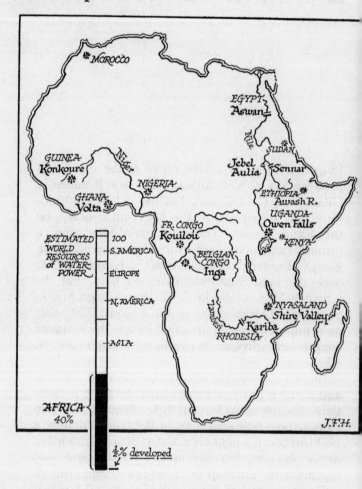

Morocco

EGYPT
Aswan

Nile

GUINEA
Konkoure

Niger

SUDAN
Jebel
Aulia   Sennar

NIGERIA

ETHIOPIA
Awash R.

GHANA
Volta

UGANDA
Owen Falls

FR. CONGO
Kouilou

KENYA

ESTIMATED
WORLD
RESOURCES
of WATER-
POWER

100
S. AMERICA

EUROPE

BELGIAN
CONGO
Inga

N. AMERICA

ASIA

NYASALAND
Shire Valley

Zambesi

Kariba
RHODESIA

J.F.H.

AFRICA
40%

½% developed

WATER AND WATER-POWER

AFRICA, IT IS estimated, has 40% of the water-power of the globe. Less than $\frac{1}{2}$% has so far been developed. Yet water, as a scientist has pointed out,[1] "is scanty in at least three-quarters of Africa south of the Sahara, and it would be no exaggeration to say that in more than half of the region water is the principal factor limiting all forms of human endeavour."

The map shows some of the principal centres of hydro-electric power, actually working or projected. As will be noted, the four great rivers—Nile, Niger, Congo and Zambesi—all come into this picture. The damming of these rivers not only means electric power, but water for irrigation; and it may be mentioned here that African agricultural production has increased by over half in the last twenty years, well above the world's average increase.

A scheme which might have had revolutionary results all over Africa was the Tanganyika Ground Nut Scheme (1947), which, "in spite of the failure of its main objective," says the scientist already quoted, "did much scientific work of a pioneering character."

[1] E. B. Worthington, *Science in the Development of Africa.*

MAP 47

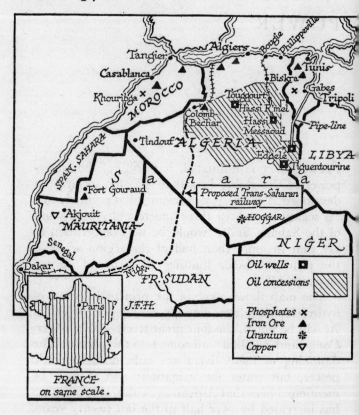

Tangier
Algiers
Bougie
Philippeville
Casablanca
Tunis
Biskra
Khouribga ✕
MOROCCO
Gabes
Tripoli
Touggourt
Hassi R'mel
Colomb-Béchar
Hassi Messaoud
Pipe-line
Tindouf
ALGERIA
SPAN. SAHARA
Edgelé
LIBYA
Tiguentourine
S   a   h   a   r   a
Fort Gouraud
Proposed Trans-Saharan railway
✱ HOGGAR
▽ Akjouit
MAURITANIA
NIGER
Senegal
Dakar
Niger
FR. SUDAN
J.F.H.

Oil wells ▣
Oil concessions ▨
Phosphates ✕
Iron Ore ▲
Uranium ✱
Copper ▽

Paris

FRANCE
on same scale.

OPENING UP THE SAHARA

One unsolved question on which scientists are working is whether the dessication of the Sahara has yet ceased—whether it and its surrounding regions are drying up still further. However that may be the Sahara has recently been found to contain liquid of another sort, a sort especially valuable in the world today—oil. In eastern Algeria oil-wells are actually in production at Hassi Messaoud, Edgelé, and Tiguentourine. A pipeline connects the former with Touggourt, railhead of a line from Edgelé and Gabes, in Tunisia. Oil is being searched for in a wide area (see map).

Iron is also being worked, and uranium has been discovered in the Hoggar, the volcanic massif in the very centre of the Sahara.

MAP 48

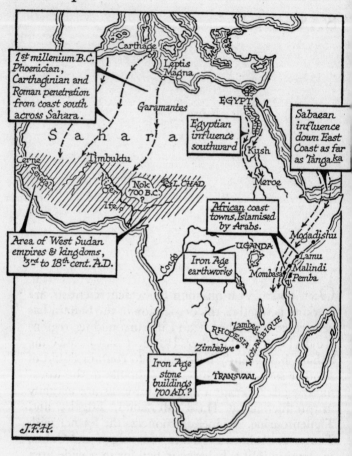

1ˢᵗ millenium B.C.
Phoenician,
Carthaginian and
Roman penetration
from coast south
across Sahara.

Carthage

Leptis
Magna

EGYPT

Garamantes

S a h a r a

Egyptian
influence
southward

Kush

Sabaean
influence
down East
Coast as far
as Tanga ka

Cerne
Senegal

Timbuktu

Niger

Nok
700 B.C.
?

Ife

L. CHAD

Meroe

Area of West Sudan
empires & kingdoms,
3ʳᵈ to 18ᵗʰ cent. A.D.

African coast
towns, Islamised
by Arabs.

Mogadishu

Congo

UGANDA

Iron Age
earthworks

Lamu
Malindi
Mombasa
Pemba

Zambesi

RHODESIA

Zimbabwe

Iron Age
stone
buildings
700 A.D.?

TRANSVAAL

MOZAMBIQUE

J.F.H.

118

DIGGING UP AFRICA'S PAST

THE AFRICA OF the future will know a great deal more about the Africa of the past. Although relatively little systematic excavation has been done, archaeologists have already proved that Africa is extremely rich in evidences of the Stone Age, the Neolothic and the Iron Ages. (And "archaeology in this letterless continent," remarks Basil Davidson, "is concerned with 'pre-history' right up to the 18th century.") Until recently, moreover, neither primitive Africans nor civilised (?) settlers showed much respect for the remains of ancient cultures, some rock-paintings, according to E. B. Worthington, having been used for 0·22 rifle practice.

The map shows a few of the main areas and objectives on which archaeological work has begun, or is planned.

MAP 49

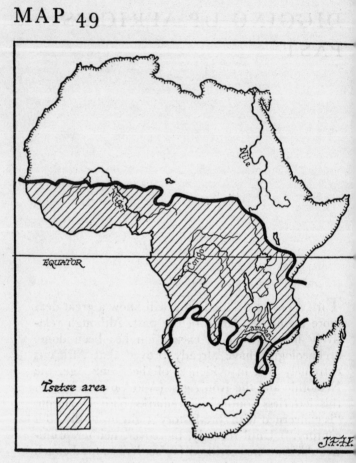

EQUATOR

Nile

Niger

Congo

Zambesi

Tsetse area

J.F.H.

MOSQUITO AND TSETSE

Two of man's deadliest enemies in Africa—much more dangerous than lions, rhinosceri or buffalo—are insects: the malaria mosquito and the tsetse-fly. "The mosquito is bad enough," writes Sir Julian Huxley,[1] but malaria does not drive cultivation out of a country like the fly-disease of cattle, nor does it kill humans wholesale, like the tsetse, by sleeping-sickness. . . . And there is not merely one, but half a dozen kinds of tsetse-fly;[2] and several of them will convey the trypanosomes of cattle disease or of sleeping-sickness with complete impartiality, either separately or both at once. Tsetse live largely on game. But you cannot, even if you wanted to, exterminate all the game in the country. . . . Tsetse live chiefly in bush. But you cannot readily destroy tracts of bush as big as France."

The map shows the Tsetse Belt. But there are areas within it free from the fly, which is unable to live in high altitudes (anything over 2,000 metres) or in grassy or cultivated areas, free from bush, or in dense forest. . . . Laboratories in Europe as well as in Africa are working intensively on tsetse control.

A note on the mosquito: "The most dangerous agency for carrying mosquitoes or the diseases they transmit about the world today," E. B. Worthington reminds us, "is the aeroplane."

[1] *Africa View*.   [2] E. B. Worthington says there are twenty-one.

MAP 50

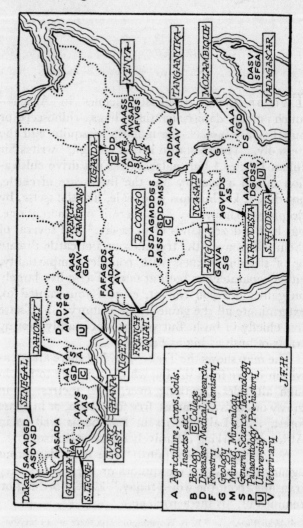

Dakar SAAADGD
ASDVSD

GUINEA AAF
AASADA

S. LEONE C

IVORY
COAST

GHANA

AAVS
AAS
A

AA AA
GD S
A

DAHOMEY

SENEGAL

NIGERIA

DADSAS
AAVFG

FRENCH
EQUAT.

FAFAGDS
DAADAAA
AV

FRENCH
CAMEROONS

AAS
ASAV
GDA

B. CONGO

DSDAGMDDGS
SASSDGDDSMSV
C

UGANDA

DD
A
AVFG
D
S

KENYA

AAASS
MVSAPD
AFVGS

TANGANYIKA

ADDMAG
AAAV

MOZAMBIQUE

AAA
VGD

DS

ANGOLA

GAVA
SG

NYASA-LD

AGVFDS
AS

A
G

N. RHODESIA

AAAAA
DGDSS
A V

S. RHODESIA

MADAGASCAR

DASV
SFGA

A Agriculture, Crops, Soils.
  Insects, etc.
B Biology   C College
D Diseases, Medical research,
F Forestry   Chemistry
G Geology
M Mining, Mineralogy
S General Science, Technology
P Palaeontology, Pre-history,
  University
V Veterinary

J.F.H.

SCIENCE, SCIENCE, SCIENCE . . .

This, although not all African nationalists may realise it, is perhaps the most important map in this book. It shows, in a cross-central section of the continent, the scientific work now being done—the institutes, research stations, technical services operating in the several territories, roughly classified in their various groups.

What each initial letter represents may be gauged by two or three specimen descriptions from the list given by E. B. Worthington in his *Science in the Development of Africa*:—

Belgian Congo: *Comité Special du Katanga*, Elizabethville. 45 scientists. Cartography, geology and mining, hydrology, agriculture, forestry and animal production.

Ivory Coast: *Institut d'Enseignment et des Recherches Tropicales*. 13 scientists. Botany, agricultural and medical entomology.

Rhodesia: *Grasslands Agricultural Research Station*. 9 scientists. Pasture research and animal husbandry.

Mozambique: *Missao de Combate as Tripanosomiasis*. 21 scientists. Human and animal trypanosomiasis and tsetse flies. With 3 sub-stations for entomological work and 5 for the control of disease.

This is the work which is going to enable Africa to take its place in the 20th-century world. And note: *some of these scientists are Africans, and their number is increasing.*

INDEX

The numbers are of maps, but the entries refer to the letterpress opposite the map as well as to the map itself.